SCAMMERS BLACK SECRETE

ULTIMATE GUIDE TO DETECTING SCAMMERS.

FRANK ZAPATA

Table of content

Black secrete methods for identifying a con artist. 2

What to Do If You've Been Scammed 3

How to recognize a scam and its warning signs 5

Common types of scam to watch for 7

How to Spot Fake Emails and Phishing Scams 10

How to spot a phishing email or text 12

Money Transfer Scams 23

How to spot & avoid conveyancing fraud 26

CEO fraud 27

Mandate fraud 29

Bank fraud alerts 32

How to spot & avoid bank fraud alert scams 33

Social Media Scams 35

Ray Ban adverts 44

Virus spreading 46

Online Dating Fraud 48

Spotting a fraudster 49

Send no intimate pictures of yourself. 53

Dig deeper 54

Offline Scams 59

Courier fraud 60

ATM skimmers 62

Tech support phone scam 64

Door-to-door Scam **65**

Scam mail & offers **67**

Crash for cash **68**

Conclusion **70**

In addition to advice on what to do if you become the victim of a scam, here are three methods for identifying a con artist.

1. The individual claims to work for a company you recognize.
2. A sense of urgency exists.
3. There's a Strange Request for an Initial Payment

Scammers are getting smarter these days, but it's still possible to spot scams and protect yourself from falling for them. Similar red flags, such as a sense of urgency or a request for money, are common in common scams; recognizing these signs can assist you in identifying fraud before it occurs. In addition to advice on what to do if you become the victim of a scam,

Here are three methods for identifying a con artist.

1. The Person Pretends to Be an Employee of a Company You Know In a typical con, a con artist may contact you and request private information by claiming to be an employee of a retail establishment you frequent, the IRS, your employer, or another organization you are familiar with. In an effort to obtain personal information from you, such as your Social Security number, bank account number, or password, they may create a fictitious email address or phone number that appears to be yours. They may then contact you via phone, email, or text message.

These tricksters may likewise endeavor to introduce malware on your PC or gadget to collect private data and passwords, so try not to tap on any connections or download connections assuming that you feel a little skeptical about the shipper. Check the email header to ensure that the sender is who they claim to be if you receive messages that seem unusual or inappropriate. Instead of responding to their message, contact the organization or company directly if you are unsure of the legitimacy of a phone number or email address. Also, keep in mind that government agencies like the Internal Revenue Service (IRS) and the Social Security Administration will only ever get in touch with you by mail in the United States. They will never call you to ask for money or personal information.

2. There's a Sense of Urgency Swindlers often try to convince people to act quickly to fix a problem that doesn't really exist because fear is a powerful motivator. Tricksters might attempt to persuade you there is an issue you should settle immediately, for example, by sending cash to an in general prison or giving a Visa

number to an alleged service organization planning to end your administration. If someone calls and tells you to "act fast," tell them you'll call back and verify the request through the appropriate channels. Don't talk to the potential con artist, even if you just want to answer their questions. Doing so could make you more involved in the con.

3. Scammers may claim that you need to make a payment in order to get access to opportunities like housing or employment. There is an unusual request for upfront payment. For instance, some rip-offs involving leasing apartments will require you to make a substantial down payment in order to proceed with the application or viewing of the property. In one common employment scam, you may be asked to pay for equipment before being hired, or you may be offered guaranteed or easy income if you purchase their program. Swindlers in the lottery may make the claim that you have won a prize, but in order to collect it, you must pay a fee. You might also be asked to send money to a con artist in unusual ways, like with gift cards, peer-to-peer payments, wire transfers, or cryptocurrency. These kinds of payment requests are a big red flag because they can be difficult to track (and recover).Make sure you know the person you are doing business with or have a reliable way to confirm their identity and their request if you are hesitant about exchanging money.

What to Do If You've Been Scammed

If you've been scammed, the following are some options for dealing with the situation:

• Get in touch with your credit card and bank.

Your bank and credit card companies can immediately cancel your cards and send you new ones if your credit card information is used in a scam. They are also able to check your most recent transactions and flag any purchases that are bogus. You won't be held liable for any unauthorized charges made with your account if the issuer of your credit card has a zero-liability guarantee. Your liability for credit card fraud is limited to $50 under federal law.

•Contact the credit authorities.

Contact the three consumer credit bureaus Experian, TransUnion, and Equifax to restrict access to your credit reports in the event that you believe someone has gained access to your personally identifiable information. To limit access and protect yourself, you can freeze your credit or place a fraud alert on your credit reports.

• Get in touch with authorities.

Law enforcement may be able to assist you, or at least use your experience to help others avoid scams similar to yours, depending on the type of scam. You can report it to the police in your area or to the official sites for fraud and identity theft run by the Federal Trade Commission.

• Change the passwords you use online.

A hacker may be able to access other accounts if they gain access to one of your passwords. All of your accounts should have unique passwords so that even if a hacker knows one, the others won't be compromised.

If you think a con artist might have gotten your personal information, you should take steps to cut down on your losses. To protect yourself from identity theft and fraud, in addition to the steps outlined above, you might want to think about signing up for a free credit monitoring service or identity theft protection service.

How to recognize a scam and its warning signs

Humans are susceptible to being conned for a variety of reasons. We have a natural desire to assist others, are curious, want to be liked, and are frequently lazy. Additionally, we are conditioned to want to trust one another. Fraudsters are aware of this and employ it against us. As a result, the majority of frauds will share some characteristics. Be suspicious of anyone you don't know if they show any of the following signs—it could save you a lot of money!

1) Strange payment requests Requiring an upfront payment, changing bank information, or paying through a money transfer service are all potential red flags.

2) Authority Fraudsters will pretend to be in authority by impersonating well-known businesses, banks, government agencies, lawyers, or even the police.

3) Urgency Scammers may try to get you to act quickly out of panic because they know that the faster you act, the less time you have to figure out it's a scam.

4) "Don't tell anyone": The less people who are aware, the less likely it is that someone will find out that it is a con and let others know.

5) Playing with your feelings Scams frequently play with our feelings, particularly curiosity, empathy, hope, panic, an lottery

6) Sounds too good to be true. It almost always is if something seems too good to be true (sorry, you haven't won that lottery!)

Now, not all of these characteristics will be present in every scam, at least one will almost certainly be.

And not all of them come suddenly or from strangers; Some fraudsters, like dating fraudsters who may attempt to build trust over time, take their time waiting for the right time to strike.

Common types of scam to watch for

Scams can take many different forms and have many different effects on their victims. We've gathered some of the most common scams used by criminals here. Understanding how some of these scams operate can help us recognize other scams.

Email scams

Scams in email: In addition to phishing emails, there are a lot of other types of scams to be on the lookout for, such as attachments with viruses and links to fake banking websites.

Email has become a very popular tool for fraudsters due to its ease of hiding the true sender, which has led to the proliferation of numerous scams.

Spotting email scams Just consider how many emails you respond to daily:

The usual messages from friends?

Requests from your supervisor?

Emails with special deals from businesses you already do business with?

We routinely follow up on email without addressing it.

Now, consider what would occur if a con artist sent you an email that, by chance, resembled something you might have expected. It only takes one email to look "normal" and get past your defenses to cost you a lot of money. Sadly, this is why you need to always be aware that any email could be a scam.

You should examine an email more closely if you notice any of the following:

What is phishing?

Never rely on the sender's name to be genuine when sending text messages because the sender can easily be faked (for example, ("UK Gov").

Criminals send phishing emails and text messages to thousands of unrelated individuals with the intention of stealing financial or other confidential information.

They might send you to a fictitious website where they ask for your personal information, or they might send you an attachment that, when you open it, installs a virus or other malware on your computer.

Phishing is most frequently associated with emails, but it can also be sent via text message (sometimes referred to as "smashing") or even recorded phone calls ("vising").

How to Spot Fake Emails and Phishing Scams

Phishing messages are so named because they are malicious spam that is sent to thousands of people at random in the hope that someone will bite. This is analogous to dangling a hook into a pond full of fish.

Phishing emails are frequently used by criminals to spread computer viruses and try to get our personal information and passwords.

Help! I Opened A Phishing Email Or Text

Phishing scams typically fall into one of two categories: malicious attachments with viruses and other malware or links to fictitious websites that attempt to steal your personal information.

From time to time, phony text messages or emails can easily fool us all. If you have opened a phishing email or clicked on a link that looks suspicious, the next steps to take are outlined in detail below.

If you opened an attachment in a phishing email...

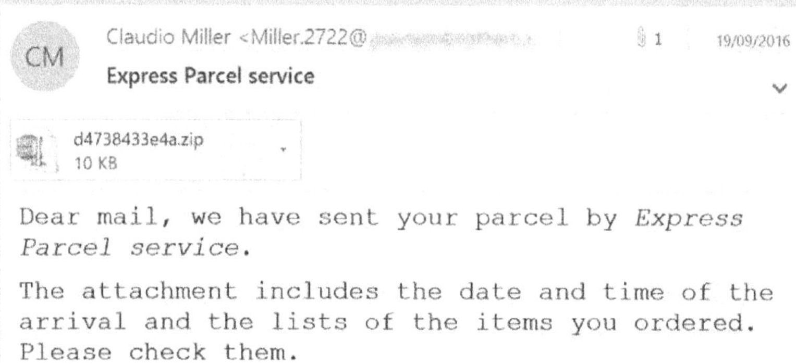

An unexpected attachment - likely to be loaded with viruses!

Phishing emails with malicious attachments that contain malware and viruses are a common type.

These could come in the form of a delivery note, an invoice, or something else to get you to open it.

Even if the file opens normally and looks like the document it claims to be, that doesn't mean it's not fake. The file may even have been designed to look legitimate when opened to reduce suspicion.

If a message asking you to "Enable Macros" appears when you open it, for instance, this could be one of the signs that it is infected; however, to be on the safe side, it is best to always assume the worst and perform the steps listed below.

How to spot a phishing email or text

The design and quality of phishing scams vary greatly. Some are obvious immediately without requiring further investigation, while others can be more subtle and clever. However, the good news is that most phishing scams are easy to spot if you know what to look for.

The most typical warning signs of a phishing email are listed on this page; the majority will have at least one of the following characteristics:

Warning signs of a phishing email:

- **Unexpected**
- **Web links that don't match**
- **Sense of urgency or worry**
- **Attachment**
- **Poorly written**
- **Impersonal**
- **An unusual "From" address**

1. Unexpected

AccountsPayable@

Remittance Advice

6134443_101115_1418...
84 KB

Dear Sir/Madam,

Please find attached your remittance advice.

Regards,
NCC

I'm not expecting any payment from this company...

The majority of phishing attacks are spread at random. Even if a message appears to be from a company with which you have an account, its unexpectedness should always cause you to question it.

Always stop and ask:

Is this the expected message?

It's probably a scam if it's for a delivery you didn't expect, a product you didn't buy, a payment you weren't due, or an invoice you didn't know about.

Do you even know who or what the message is intended to come from?

BT

Cyber Breaches

Dear BT Customer,

Due to security breaches on an international scale. BT have launched preventative measures in ensuring your customer data remains safe.

BT have been busy upgrading our security to keep your personal details safe. To do this in the most secure way possible, we have temporarily limited access to profile features that contain your sensitive data. To confirm your security upgrade and reestablish full access to your BT account please follow the link below

Confirm security upgrade

Deficiency to do so will result in limited access to your profile.

Need more help?

Please don't reply to this email as we won't get your message. If you've got any questions, or for more ways to get in touch, go to bt.com/help

Thanks for choosing BT.
Libby Barr
Managing Director, Customer Care

A phishing email taking advantage of the global Winery *outbreak.*

As is the case with the current pandemic of the coronavirus, some con artists also take advantage of significant news events to stage their con schemes. Numerous con artists have taken on the guise of organizations like the World Health Organization (WHO) or your local health service to offer dubious advice, phony treatments, or even the vaccine.

Making it appear as though the attack came from someone you know is one way that phishing attempts are made to appear legitimate:

Scammers may send emails to all of a person's friends by hijacking their email accounts.

It is possible to control who appears to be sending text messages.

Never give a message your trust just because it says it's from someone or an organization you know!

If you ever receive anything unusual from a friend or organization, you should always call them to find out if they actually sent it. This is much simpler than recovering from a virus or scam.

To open attachments or click on links, criminals rely on our natural curiosity. Always pause to reflect!

2. Web links that don't match the website

http://prime2.online-order-amazon.prod21uk.co.uk/updateaccount/index.php
Click or tap to follow link.

If you have not made this purchase visit our Help page for full refund.

We hope to see you again soon.
Amazon.co.uk

Be careful – it might be easy to assume that this link goes to Amazon, but it actually goes to "prod21uk.co.uk

Web links that do not correspond to the anticipated destination are one of the biggest indicators that a message is not genuine.

The actual location of a link in an email may not always be obvious. Hover your mouse over any email link to locate it.You should be able to see the destination of this link either in a small pop-up or at the bottom (sometimes bottom-left) of your email program. Is the address in line with your expectations?

Anything that doesn't point to a known website is a suspicious link.

For instance, if you get an email or text message that says it's from "Acme Bank," the link should take you to the company's own website, like acmebank.com.

Links should never point to a random-looking website like sdbryjddvsrg.ru. Look out for subtle differences like "acme-security.com" or "acmebankalerts.com" that could be a scam.

Links that make use of a shortening service (like bity.ly, TinyURL, or tiny.cc) should also be treated with extreme caution because these services can be used to conceal a web link's actual destination.

The best thing you can do is manually type their web address into the browser bar (not the one in the email) and log in to your account that way if the email claims to be from a company with which you already have an account.

Never click on a link if you aren't absolutely sure about it.

3. A sense of urgency or worry

To Whom It May Concern,

I got this last week, but i think it's for you.
Fine increases soon, you should take care of it ASAP.
PARKING TICKET 73842923

This is trying to panic me into clicking the link

To convince clients to tap on a web connection or open connections hoodlums will frequently provide the message with a need to get going, make stress, or just attempt to take advantage of our regular interest.

Does the message imply that ignoring it could result in financial loss? For instance, is it claiming a security issue with your account or is it sending you an email with a link to cancel an order you didn't place?

Is it implying that if you don't act, a court summons or the closure of a bank or other account are possible outcomes?

Does it prey on your curiosity, such as wanting to know who might be sending you an invoice or an unexpected package?

In order to convince us to fall for their scams, criminals use a variety of human traits, such as panic, greed, curiosity, the fear of missing out, or simply a desire to assist others. You have every right to be suspicious of the message if any of these emotional pulls are utilized.

Dear mail, we have sent your parcel by *Express Parcel service*.

The attachment includes the date and time of the arrival and the lists of the items you ordered. Please check them.

4. An email attachment

An unexpected attachment - likely to be loaded with viruses!

Many malicious emails aim to spread malware by tricking you into opening an attachment that downloads a virus to your computer.

These types of attacks are common:

- Counterfeit solicitations;
- Absent notification of packages;
- Claims that you are owed money;
- False confirmations of bookings.

Never open an attachment that you weren't expecting or aren't absolutely certain about!

The golden rule is to simply not open an attachment that you weren't expecting, regardless of whether it's a Word document, PDF, zip file, or spreadsheet.

5. Poorly written

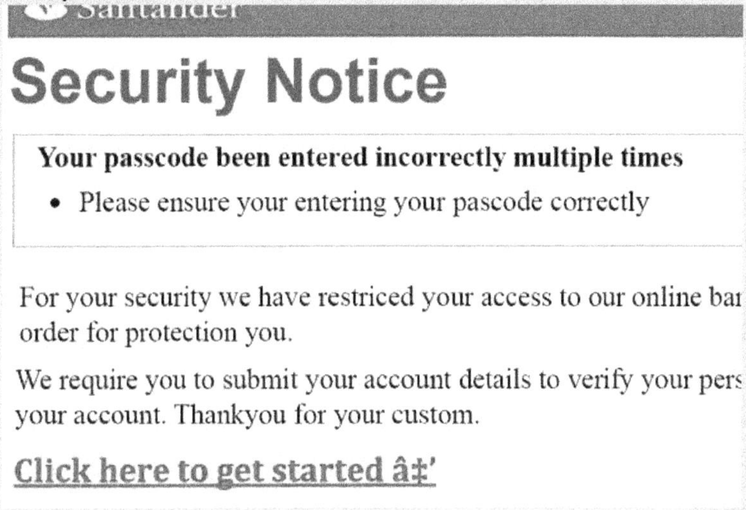

Santander

Security Notice

Your passcode been entered incorrectly multiple times

- Please ensure your entering your pascode correctly

For your security we have restriced your access to our online bai order for protection you.

We require you to submit your account details to verify your pers your account. Thankyou for your custom.

Click here to get started â‡'

Major corporations would produce professional looking emails - and use spell check!

A significant amount of cybercrime originates from nations where English is not the native tongue. Although some phishing messages may appear credible and professional, this is not always the case; any errors in grammar or spelling are always obvious indicators.

- Is there any grammatical or spelling errors in the email or text?
- Does it appear that the layout is sloppy and badly formatted?

6. Impersonal

The majority of phishing scams are generic and do not contain any personal information due to their bulk.

Is the message simply addressed to a standard “Dear customer”?

Does it include any additional personal information? Many legitimate businesses that are aware of security will try to show that the message is genuine by including something personal to you that is not public knowledge, like your account number’s last four digits.

Keep in mind, however, that this is not a foolproof method for identifying fake emails because some businesses continue to address emails in a generic manner (for instance, Amazon frequently just says “Hello”), while others will personalize their phishing messages by utilizing data stolen from other sources (for instance, some scams quote the individual’s password that has been taken from a hacked website).

Yet, the hello utilized can in any case add to a general sensation of regardless of whether to trust the message. For instance, if a message claims to be from a company that would normally address you personally, the fact that it does not include your name should always set off alarm bells.

7. An unusual "From" address

Why would Apple be sending me an invoice from Shaw in Canada?

Who transmitted the message? From addresses can be easily spoofed, so never put your faith in them, even if they appear to be genuine (this is true for both emails and text messages).

However, if the “From” address does not come from the same company that the message claims to be from, this immediately raises suspicions; likewise, if the criminals have not even attempted to conceal this, it is a foregone conclusion!

Money Transfer Scams

“Earning” money is the most common strategy employed by con artists to con us. Additionally, tricking us into transferring thousands of dollars directly into their bank account is the quickest way to accomplish this.

In recent years, money transfer scams have become increasingly common, whether the goal is to impersonate a solicitor and steal someone’s house deposit or to deceive company accountants into thinking they are a legitimate supplier who needs to be paid.

Some of the most common scams to avoid are as follows:

- **House Deposit (Conveyancing) Fraud**
- **CEO Fraud**
- **Mandate Fraud**
- **Bank Fraud Alert Scams**

1. Conveyancing fraud

The most significant purchase most of us will ever make is purchasing a home. It's energizing yet distressing in equivalent measure, with colossal amounts of cash evolving hands.

Conveyancing fraud has become more prevalent in recent years, and criminals have taken an interest in it due to the large sums of money involved.

Criminals send fake emails pretending to be from the buyer's lawyer here, giving the buyer the wrong bank information to send their deposit to.

Frequently crooks accomplish this by hacking into the specialist's email account, observing all correspondence among purchaser and specialist, and afterward (when all is good and well) acting like the specialist to send messages from this authentic record. This kind of fraud is extremely cruel, but it works so well that it kills people. A lot of money is often lost and never found.

How to spot & avoid conveyancing fraud

By simply double-checking the bank information, this fraud can be avoided easily. Never rely on email to confirm anything because the scammers might be in charge of your lawyer's email account. The best method is usually a quick phone call to your lawyer.

A straightforward call could help try not to lose your life investment funds.

What to do if you're caught out?

It may be difficult to spot this fraud because it originates from your solicitor's actual email account. If this happens to you, you should do the following:

- **Explain the situation to your bank right away and ask them to freeze any payments that haven't been processed yet. Contact their fraud unit; They might be able to get some of the money back after they start an investigation.**

- **Inform the police about the con.Get the investigator's contact information and a crime reference number.**

- **Immediately inform your attorney about this. Don't use email because the criminals might still have access to it; instead, call them up. They will need to immediately restore the security of their email account and notify all of their other clients.**

CEO fraud

Weds 12/10/2016 1:23 PM

David Holsworthy <david.holsworthy@ >

RE: Urgent

Hi Gareth,

Are you free at the moment? I'm in a meeting all afternoon but need to process a money transfer to one of our suppliers ASAP. Let me know that you're able to do this & I'll send you the account details.

David

A typical "CEO Fraud" email

In this con, the criminal pretends to be a company CEO or other senior director and sends an email to a member of the finance team requesting an urgent transfer of a large sum of money. It is very specific; the criminals might even have access to the CEO's email account or be using an email address that looks very similar to it.

Sadly, these scams are very successful, costing some businesses millions of dollars and costing some people their jobs. Between October 2013 and February 2016, this kind of fraud was reported to have caused more than $2.3 billion in losses to US law enforcement.

How to spot & avoid CEO fraud

If you ever receive this type of email:

- **Always challenge the request. Don't just go along with it until you've tried other methods, like calling or talking to your CEO in person, to make sure it's real.**
- **Avoid putting yourself under pressure. Use your judgment and follow the procedures of your company; numerous fraudsters attempt to pressure you into acting rapidly before have opportunity and energy to understand it's a trick.**

What checks and procedures does your company have in place if you are a member of the finance team? Would a single director's email be sufficient to initiate a small cash transfer? How do you check the details of any requests or banks? Reviewing your procedures and processes is worthwhile!

What to do if you're caught out?

- **Call your bank right away; Explain the situation to them and request that any unconfirmed payments be frozen. Contact their fraud unit; They might be able to get some of the money back after they start an investigation.**

- **Check with your CEO—or the alleged sender—to determine whether the email was actually sent. Contact them by phone or in person to accomplish this; Email shouldn't be trusted because criminals might still have access to it.**

- **Inform the police about the con.Get the investigator's contact information and a crime reference number.**

- **The email account's password should be changed immediately by your CEO.Your IT team should also look into whether their email account has been hacked.**

Mandate fraud

Mandate fraud occurs when a person pretends to be one of your current suppliers and convinces you to change the bank information used to pay them.

This kind of fraud is committed by a wide range of businesses, from small to large, and it can deceive even large corporations. It's basically a different kind of conveyancing fraud, but this time it's targeting businesses instead.

In some cases this extortion is completed by the hoodlums emulating the email address of the organization they're acting like; In other instances, they have actually gained complete control by hacking into the company's email.It's not just limited to email; it has also been reported to have been carried out via postal service with forged company letterhead.

How to spot & avoid mandate fraud

If you ever get a request to change your payment information from someone, like a lawyer, a supplier for your business, or even just a magazine subscription, you have the following rights:

- **Even if there is no reason to believe the request is not genuine, always double-check it.**

- **Never rely on email to get in touch with them again; keep in mind that the hackers might be in charge of their email account. A quick phone call**

from a phone number you know to be accurate is frequently the best method.

What to do if you're caught out?

If you think you might have been scammed like this, you need to act quickly if you want to get your money back:

- **Call your bank right away; Explain the situation to them and request that any unconfirmed payments be frozen. Contact their fraud unit; They might be able to get some of the money back after they start an investigation.**

- **Verify the authenticity of the email's sender by speaking with the supplier it purports to be from. Make this call; email shouldn't be trusted if the criminals still have access to it.**

- **Inform the police about the con.Get the investigator's contact information and a crime reference number.**

- **Ensure that anyone else in your company who has the authority to change payment details is aware that this happened; they'll need to be on the lookout for any further attempts the fraudsters may make.**

Bank fraud alerts

There are numerous variations of this scam, all of which involve the perpetrator posing as your bank or the police and claiming that your account has been hacked.

The con artists will attempt to persuade you to comply with their requests in order to safeguard yourself by emailing or (more frequently) calling you. You might be asked to do one or more of these:

- **Move your money to a "safe" account that they will explain to you;**
- **Confirm your PIN with them;**

- **Take out some cash and give it to a courier who will drop it off at your house, along with your bank card;**
- **To assist the police in identifying counterfeit goods, purchase an expensive item, such as a watch, and then hand it over to a courier who will forward it to the police.**

Several different versions are actually in use, which is not surprising! You lose a lot of money as a result of all of them. The con artists will sometimes even make the claim that bank employees are the subject of an investigation; a strategy intended to prevent you from visiting your branch where the trick may be uncovered.

Another tactic that con artists sometimes employ to win your trust is to ask you to hang up and call back using the phone number on the back of your bank card.Then you might think you're talking to your bank, but you aren't!

In many nations, a phone call only ends when both parties hang up. Therefore, even if you end the call and dial a new number, you will still be on the same call **if the** con artists don't hang up as quickly. They might counterfeit foundation commotions from a call community and have a partner dominate, yet it'll in any case be the very group of thugs that you're conversing with – not your bank.

How to spot & avoid bank fraud alert scams

If you ever get a phone call or email claiming to be from the police or your bank:

- **Be skeptical: If your bank or the police send you an email with a security alert,**

- **Never call back from the same phone after you hang up; always use a different one to call them back. Wait an hour or call a friend whose voice you recognize if you don't have another phone. Only make calls to reputable numbers, such as those on your bank card.**
- **Never divulge private information: You will never be asked for your PIN number verbally or by typing it into your phone by the police or your bank. If anyone ever inquires about this, hang up and inform the police.**
- **Never give anything to someone who knocks on your door—the police and banks will never ask for it.**

If you have any elderly or vulnerable relatives then discuss this with them and make them aware of what to do; vulnerable people living alone are often targeted in this type of scam.

What to do if you're caught out?

If you have been conned, you shouldn't feel bad about it; all people have a few normal qualities that make us powerless to misrepresentation. It is ingrained in us to want to assist others and to trust one another. Fraudsters are aware of this and employ it against us.

- **Use the phone number on the back of your bank card to immediately notify your bank that you have been taken advantage of; Explain the situation to them and request that any unconfirmed payments be frozen. Contact their fraud unit; they'll send off an examination and could possibly recuperate a portion of the cash.**
- **Inform the police about the con.Get the investigator's contact information and a crime reference number.**

- **When reporting something, make sure you know who you are talking to; be aware of the aforementioned phone line trick. Use only trusted phone numbers.**

Social Media Scams

Fraudsters frequently use social media. We trust our friends, so we are more likely to be influenced by them than by complete strangers, so it is an obvious tool for criminals to use.

Social media scams can be varied, whether they're just simple hoaxes, 'like' farming, or something more malicious. We've listed some of the more common scams below to show what to watch out for, and how you can respond.

- **Fake competitions**
- **Friend spoofing**
- **Hoax messages**
- **Ray Ban adverts**
- **Spreading viruses**

BULLYING & GROOMING

Virtual Entertainment might give joy to many, however for others it very well may be a hopeless or perilous spot.

Parents need to be aware of the dangers of bullying and grooming as well, despite the fact that this page focuses on mischief-making and money-making scams. For this reason, we recommend following the **NSPCC's** advice.

Common social media scams

Fake competitions

A fake competition, supposedly from Thomas Cook Holidays

On social media, fake competitions are common. They seem so simple to enter, and they make us dream.

These posts appear to be from well-known brands offering extravagant prizes like gift cards, free phones, or flights.

On Facebook, they appear as posts requesting your like, share, and comment, whereas on messaging apps like WhatsApp or Facebook Messenger, they frequently appear as a link to a website sent by a friend.

Who's behind these?

More often than not there's a financial motive behind these. Those that spread through messaging apps are often trying to entice people to visit a phishing website to capture personal details; for Facebook and Twitter, the aim is often to gather as many likes or retweets as possible, before selling control of the account to someone who wants a huge ready-made audience.

Entrants to these fake Facebook competitions may also be sent private messages asking them to confirm their identity, for example by sending over their credit card details.

How to spot these?

It's usually true when something seems too good to be true! However, there is a problem with the fact that a lot of small businesses occasionally conduct legitimate competitions as forms of advertising.

Therefore, how can you distinguish genuine ones from fake ones?

- **The blue tick Check the name of the account to see if it has a blue "verified" tick or an emoji on Snapchat—all official accounts do.**
- **Known as: Examine the account name to see if it differs from the genuine brand in any way. Has a full stop been added? Has an additional word, such as "Holidays" or "Shop," been used?**
- **History of accounts: Check that account's other posts; although there may be a few that give the impression that it is genuine, scroll quite far back. The average age of these accounts is just a few days.**
- **Phishing is a danger: If you don't really know where a link in a message will take you, don't click on it.**
- **Personal information: Never give out your credit card or personal information as part of a competition!**

Friend spoofing

Spoofing friends is a new but growing trend. A con artist will impersonate a person on social media, create a new account with their name and photo, and then send new friend requests to everyone on that person's friends list in this con.

The con artist will attempt to have a conversation with anyone who accepts the request, possibly assuming that their friend had a technical issue and is simply reconnecting. They'll try to "phish" for personal information or even pretend to be stranded abroad and ask for a loan in order to take advantage of the victim's trust (they'll think they're talking to a friend).

How can I spot these?

Be wary if you receive a request for a connection from a friend you already know. Your suspicions may be bolstered by differences in language, inaccurate facts, or even just your gut feeling.

If you are suspicious, you should never divulge a lot of personal information and never transfer any money (no matter how convincing the story!).Try contacting your friend in a different way, like by email, to make sure it's really them. If that is not an option, gently test how well they know about your friendship or look at their profile.

If you ever come across a fake account, you should notify the person whose account has been copied, any friends, and the social media platform they are using. It only takes a small number of victims for fraudsters to succeed.

How can I stop my account being cloned?

Fraudsters will only clone accounts they can fully view and learn about to increase their chances of fooling people. Adjust your privacy settings to ensure that your friends list is hidden from public view and that this is not you.

Hoax messages

+44 1234 123456 ~Ernst Blowfeld

If you know anyone using WhatsApp you might pass on this. An IT colleague has advised that a video comes out tomorrow from WhatsApp called martinelli do not open it , it hacks your phone and nothing will fix it. Spread the word. If you receive a message to update the Whatsapp to Whatsapp Gold, do not click !!!!!
Now said on the news this virus is difficult and severe

Pass it on to all

13:16

The Martinelli hoax on WhatsApp....

....and on Facebook

Not all scams are motivated by money; some are just made to cause trouble!

Any messages that warn of danger have the potential to go viral because we all want to remain safe and we also want our friends to remain safe. Sharing these makes us feel good, and we believe we are helping other people.

There are a wide variety of hoaxes, some of which have been around for years. Another warning about eggs being thrown at your car's windshield and the Martinelli hoax (see images to the right) are very common.

How to spot these?

It can be challenging to distinguish between genuine and fake news in this day and age of fake news. Messages that claim to be a warning, ones that actively

encourage us to share them with friends, and ones that are (mostly) written in poor English are all common indicators of hoaxes.

Just by searching the message's key words on the internet, many hoaxes can be proven to be fake. Are the websites real or false? Additionally, Snopes can be useful for research.

If you see one of these shared by a friend, quietly let them know that you think it's a hoax and perhaps include a link to a story that refutes it so they can remove the post. Remember that they thought they were doing you a favor by warning you, so don't laugh at them for falling for it!

Ray Ban adverts

A few variants of the Ray Ban scam.

These posts are probably familiar to you if you use Facebook or Instagram: a friend of yours posted a deal for 90% off Ray-Ban glasses to their friend's newsfeed.

The point of this trick is to draw you to their site to purchase glasses, taking your charge card subtleties all the while.

How to spot these?

Fortunately, these advertisements are easy to spot because of their straightforward layout and huge discounts—often up to 90%.Additionally, the address that they display is not the genuine Ray Ban website.

Even though these advertisements are specifically for Ray Ban, other brands can also be targeted. Be wary of any offer that you see that seems too good to be true!

How do I avoid these ads appearing on my feed?

The ads use social media accounts that have been hacked, most likely because of a virus. Reviewing your account's security settings is a good idea to keep yourself safe and prevent your account from being used to post things like these:

- **Make sure your password is strong;**
- **Your login should undergo an additional security check;**
- **Examine the apps that can access your account.**

What if my account is already spamming these?

If a friend has reported that your account is sending these, you should immediately change your password and add a second factor login to your account's security settings. You can also see who is logged in and disable their access.

Virus spreading

While you're utilizing online entertainment destinations almost certainly, you're monitor is down to some degree; After all, it stands to reason that these tech giants will prevent any malicious activity, doesn't it?

Sadly, however, that is not entirely accurate. Even though social media platforms like Twitter and Facebook put in a lot of effort to remove malicious content, some still appear. Web links that, when clicked, spread a virus to your computer are one example.

These are frequently included in posts that are meant to catch your attention. You will be taken to a malicious website when you click the link, where your phone or computer will download a virus. The page you visit might be what you expected, encouraging you to share it with your friends as well, and at first you might not notice anything amiss.

How to spot these?

A type of content known as “clickbait” is written to get your attention and encourage you to click through. They might announce a celebrity’s death, be deliberately controversial, or even entice you with a tempting competition.

If you see a post similar to this one, don’t click on it, no matter how tempting it may be. Use a search engine to determine whether or not it is true if it claims to be a breaking news story (such as a celebrity death).

Online Dating Fraud

One of the cruelest forms of fraud is dating scams, which take advantage of our most intimate feelings and have the potential to cause devastating emotional scarring.

Don't be embarrassed if this happens to you; report it and help tackle it head-on. There's no need to feel alone.

Get right to the point:

BIG BUSINESS

Action Fraud estimates that dating scams cost £41 million in the United Kingdom in 2017, with an average loss of £11,500 per victim. Additionally, this is likely to be a significant underestimate because romance fraud is a crime that is frequently thought to go unreported.

What is romance fraud?

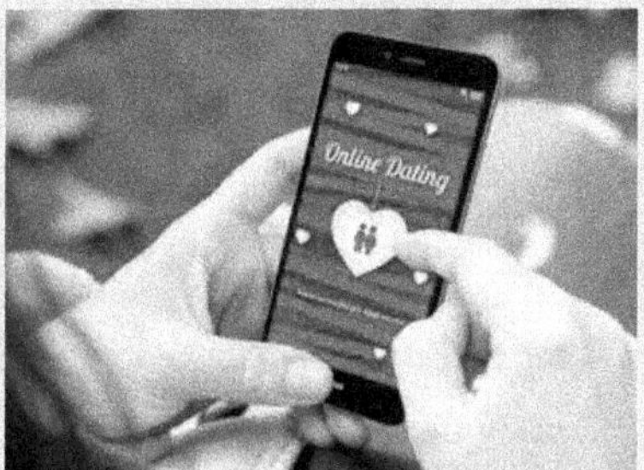

Dating scams, also known as romance scams, are a type of fraud in which criminals form online relationships with people looking for love and become friends with them before eventually taking advantage of their trust to make money.

Often, it involves tricking victims into sending money for an "emergency," but it can also involve blackmailing them over intimate photos or videos (sextortion) or getting them to transfer money or goods for the criminals without knowing it.

It is known to have the same effect on men and women.

Spotting a fraudster

Look for any of the following telltale signs if you've started an online relationship and are a little suspicious, or if you're concerned about a friend's online date:

Moving the discussion along

- Scam detection systems are standard on all reputable dating websites. Naturally, this detests fraudsters! Furthermore, attempt to rapidly move discussions onto different stages, like email or WhatsApp.

Avoiding inquiries regarding themselves

- Dating scammers talk to a lot of potential victims at once, so they don't talk much about "themselves" to avoid getting themselves in trouble. They try to avoid answering questions and instead focus on trying to make you feel special, which is nice because who doesn't like it when someone is interested in us a lot?

Inconsistencies in their statements

- It's hard to keep up a fake persona, and the con artist will occasionally make mistakes. They might say things that are completely at odds with their profile or even contradict themselves from time to time.

Are they a businessman who travels or a member of the military?

- Fraudsters frequently use these two kinds of profiles because they provide the ideal justification for not being able to meet up. It also lends credence to the urgent request for a cash transfer to assist them in returning home or receiving medical treatment abroad after being "mugged."

Too perfect?

- Is your date just too good to be true? Naturally, there are people who are almost flawless (like me, of course!) However, we all have some flaw. In order to catch our attention, criminals frequently use photographs of models or other highly attractive individuals, and their descriptions—as well as their ongoing conversations—are made up to sound as appealing as they possibly can.

soliciting private information

- Be careful about sharing private information with the person you're speaking with; They will be able to conduct more research on you the more information you provide them, shaping their persona into someone they believe you are more likely to like.
- Of course, in a real relationship, you share information, but it's a red flag if they push too hard or ask for too much too quickly.

Unwilling to communicate or meet

- All con artists realize that the game would be up assuming you at any point met face to face, and even calls can be interesting (their articulation may not be the thing you're anticipating!).As a result, they will come up with a variety of justifications to avoid speaking or meeting up.
- And even if you do manage to talk on the phone, the person on the other end may actually be in a call center made just for these scams, and your

"date" has been given notes about all of your conversations to help them stay in character. It's a big deal!

If you have doubts about a person but still want to give them the benefit of the doubt, it's fine to keep talking to them because they might be real and end up being the love of your life! Just be aware of the warning signs, avoid getting too emotionally involved with them until you meet, which is easier said than done, and never give them money. Having a friend listen to your concerns can also provide you with an objective perspective.

Prevent yourself falling victim

The con artist's ultimate objective is to defraud you. There are a few basic steps you should always take to avoid being conned, regardless of whether you think someone is a con artist or if you completely trust your online date.

Never contribute any cash.

- Never ever transfer any money to someone you have never met, no matter how tragic or emotional the sob story they tell you or how long you've been talking to them (some scams take months to work).
- You might try to justify the requests to yourself by saying, "A little money can't hurt, right?" because the initial requests for money are typically insignificant. Before expanding rapidly until you suddenly find yourself in a deep hole. It is common for fraudsters to promise that they will repay you, but that they only need this one last payment to get themselves out of a situation before they can access their money to repay you. Fraudsters are aware that once someone has given even a small amount, they are more likely to keep giving.
- The reason given will typically be an urgent loan, a medical emergency, or anything else that will make you feel bad for not helping them. They take advantage of the fact that you would find it difficult to refuse because you have already invested so much time and emotion in the relationship.
- Even if you say you don't have any money, they have prepared responses and have helped victims get credit.

Send no intimate pictures of yourself.

- The use of extortion is becoming more common. Some con artists gain your trust enough to ask for intimate photos or videos, then suddenly reveal their true identity and threaten to send it to all of your friends, colleagues, and family unless you pay a fee (sextortion).

- **Make sure you've met them first before becoming intimate, and don't give them the ability to do this.**

Don't send any money or items to them.

- **Dating websites have been used by money launderers to find money mules. Of course, the victim might not be aware that they are breaking the law, but a judge cannot use that as an excuse!**

- **Always refuse to accept any money or items that would enable you to relocate. Although their justifications may be particularly inventive, they always use them as a cover for their criminal activity. Immediately report any such requests to the police.**

Dig deeper

If you're reading this, you might already be thinking that the person you're speaking with isn't always who they say they are. Scammers frequently steal photos from online profiles and simply use profiles that they know work. The good news is that you can rely on internet search engines here!

Do a web search on their profile photo

- Photos of attractive people that they find online are used by fraudsters. The good news is that it is now simple to perform a reverse image search on the internet to determine where else the same image may be found.
- To begin, download the profile picture of your date to your computer by right-clicking on it and selecting "save as..." or "save picture as..." (it doesn't matter where on your computer you save it).
- Go to Google Images next. Click the camera icon in the search bar to upload the image from your PC.
- If you find the same photo attached to a different dating profile or to someone who is not even related to you, you should raise an alarm.

Run their profile through search engines

- Do a search on the internet for their name using keywords like "dating fraud" or "romance scam," such as "joe blogs dating scam."
- Also, try copying bits of text from their profile or messages to you and entering it into a search engine with quotation marks around it.You might find that the con artists have used the same profile information before and that other people who have been scammed are talking about them online.

- Keep in mind that the absence of any results on these searches does not necessarily indicate that they are genuine; they may have created a distinctive profile; however, if you discover any evidence against them, it is almost certain that they are a criminal.

Subtly challenge them

If you want to be subtle and challenge your date without making it clear that you suspect them, you might ask for a photo of them in a particular pose or setting (like doing their hobby) or any other photo with a special request attached that they will need to take specifically. You can make this sound romantic if you use your imagination!

If the dating profile photo they used was stolen from someone else, they won't be able to fulfill your request, and you might find them making excuses for why they can't (for instance, if they say they are in the military, they will probably say that operational secrecy prevents them from taking photos).If they don't send you this photo, this should be a big red flag.

It Is known that some con artists have stock photos of models holding up blank signs onto which they can Photoshop anything, including a message with your name on it or a head on a photo of someone else entirely. Be aware, however, of the possibility of photo shopping. Instead, request a shot of them in action or doing something unusual.

If you are being scammed...

What then should you do if you are fairly certain that your internet date is not who they claim to be?

Stop!

The obvious first step is to simply stop making payments, regardless of how much you have already paid out.

If you have recently transferred money and there is a possibility that it has not yet been processed, you should immediately contact your bank to determine whether the transaction can be stopped.

Take copies of all evidence

Make copies of all the evidence; don't delete anything because you might need it in the future.

Correspondence:

- Try to keep copies of every communication you've had with your date, whether it was via a dating website, email, text, Facebook, or WhatsApp.
- If at all possible, print copies, save screenshots, and note any contact information you have for them.

Original dating profile:

- Print a copy of your date's original profile from the dating or social media website where you met if you still have access to it.

Copy and store this evidence safely before challenging them - they'll likely close their profile and immediately delete conversations as soon as you do this.

Report them

A con artist will move on to the next victim as soon as they realize they won't get anything from you. You have an obligation to report them as soon as possible so that steps can be taken to stop others from becoming victims.

Many dating sites permit you to report somebody straightforwardly from inside their profile. If this is not the case, you can find instructions on how to report them in the website's help section.

Even though a lot of this fraud takes place overseas, it's still worth reporting it to the authorities because they can work with the dating website and other organizations to try to stop other people from falling victim to it.

Contingent upon which nation you're from will influence how you report the wrongdoing.
Here are some common organizations:

- **Scamwatch in Australia**
- **Action Fraud in the UK**
- **Netsafe in New Zealand**
- **The FBI's IC3 in the United States**
- **The AntiFraud Centre in Canada**
- **Europol in other EU nations**

Beware of follow up scams

Be on the lookout for any follow-up scams if you have lost money to romance fraud; some victims have reported being offered assistance in recouping their losses. Don't fall for it, whoever they are pretending to be; it's just another con that will get you to pay an advance fee that you won't see again. Be on your guard because they may also target you again with a different dating profile.

Offline Scams

Despite the fact that many new scams have been made possible by the internet, con artists and fraudsters have been making a living long before computers were invented..

There are a lot of scams out there, whether it's a door-to-door con artist, a phone call, or a letter sent through the mail.

The various types of offline scams are listed below

- **Courier fraud**
- **ATM skimmers**
- **Tech support phone scam**
- **Door-to-door fraud**
- **Scam mail & offers**
- **Crash-for-cash scams**

Despite the variety of scams to be on the lookout for, they all attempt to take advantage of human nature, so they share many similarities.

If you know **what to look for**, you can easily contribute to your own and your loved ones' safety.

Courier fraud

There are numerous variants of courier fraud, but in the end, they are all designed to try to convince you to give the criminals a large sum of money directly.

The criminals begin these con schemes with a phone call in which they pretend to be the police or your bank and ask for your assistance in either resolving a problem with your account or conducting an investigation into some dishonest bank employees.

This con can be carried out in a variety of ways:

- The guest might request that you pull out cash from your neighborhood office and pass it to a dispatch (subsequently the name of this trick) who'll visit your home so it very well may be utilized as proof;
- They might guarantee your bank cards are required as proof, requesting your PIN via telephone and training you to hand your cards to a dispatch (once in a while even after you've cut them up);
- In order to test their systems, they might ask you to move the money to a "safe" account.
- Or they might ask you to buy expensive things, like iTunes gift cards, and then hand them over to a courier once more.

The con artists promise to reimburse you as soon as their investigations are finished and make the claim that the money in your account could be in danger if you don't help.

How can this con be avoided?

Hang up if you ever get a call like this; it's a scam. Your bank and the police will never call to request your bank card, PIN, or cash withdrawal. **Never** distribute these.

Asking you to call back using the number on the back of your bank card is one of the tricks used to try and convince you that they are real. In point of fact, even if you hang up, the call might not end, so no matter which number you dial, you'll still be talking to the same group. Use a different phone to avoid this, or call a friend or family member to verify that the call has ended.

ATM skimmers

The devices known as cash machine skimmers are placed over the card slot of an ATM in order to steal your card information. They are made to look natural and not make people suspicious.

Frequently, there will also be a small camera for recording your PIN. On his website, the investigative journalist Brian Krebs has written a number of excellent **articles about ATM skimmers**. Many of these articles include numerous photographs that demonstrate how challenging it can be to identify ATM skimmers.

How can this con be avoided?

Always do a quick visual check of the card slot before using a cash machine to see if anything looks out of place. If you're not sure, you could even wiggle parts of the reader (don't worry, you won't break anything!).

Even if everything appears to be normal, always cover up your PIN as you enter it.

If you ever discover a suspicious device on an ATM, immediately notify the bank; if you are unable to locate any contact information, contact the police. Be on the lookout for scammers as you do this, as they may remain nearby after attaching a device.

I believe I am the victim; What ought I to do?

Because of their superiority, some skimming devices are nearly impossible to identify. Contact your bank right away if you notice any suspicious transactions on your account; they'll examine and if fitting repay you.

Tech support phone scam

The Technical Support Scam has been around for a long time. It takes the form of a random phone call that says it's from a well-known company, usually Microsoft, whose monitoring systems say they've found security problems with the victim's computer.

The caller will instruct the victim on how to locate these "errors" on their computer in order to persuade them. They are actually system messages, but to someone who isn't familiar with how computers work, they can look like serious errors, (especially if they have red crosses or exclamation points on them).

Level	Date and Time	Source	Event ID	Task Category
Information	28/01/2019 10:31:32	Service Control Manager	7040	None
Error	28/01/2019 10:15:22	DistributedCOM	10016	None
Error	28/01/2019 10:15:13	DistributedCOM	10016	None
Warning	28/01/2019 10:13:01	DNS Client Events	1014	(1014)
Error	28/01/2019 10:12:09	DistributedCOM	10016	None

These kinds of errors, which are hidden in the operating system of every computer and are perfectly normal, are frequently used by con artists to make people think there is a serious problem.

In the end, the caller offers to fix the problems for a fee, frequently asking for additional personal information like a date of birth to process the payment.

How to avoid this scam?

Simply hang up if you receive these calls! Don’t give them access to your computer, nor do you give them information about your bank or credit card.

Door-to-door Scam

Since the beginning of time on this planet, humans have traded and bargained. While most dealers tell the truth and dedicated, there are (unfortunately) a lot for whom ethics don't appear to exist.

This includes people who sell stolen goods door to door, people who take advantage of weak customers to get them to buy something they don't need, and thieves who pretend to be tradespeople to steal money while they are in the victim's home. In addition to these scams, there are numerous others.

How can you guard yourself?

It can be hard to tell who is real and who is trying to scam you when someone knocks on your door.

- **Be on guard**: Be suspicious at all times and remain vigilant; No matter how persuasive a salesperson may be, you should never let them into your home unannounced.
- **Slow down**: Be patient and resist the temptation to make snap decisions.
- **Verify ID**: Before letting someone in who claims to be an official, like your electricity company, always check their identification. Telephone the organization up to check

– don't utilize the telephone number from their ID yet go somewhere else to get this, (for example, on the web or by really taking a look at a past assertion).

Take some information and call back later if you are truly interested in anything being sold. Be suspicious, however, if anyone employs any sales strategies involving high pressure!

Always get a second estimate from someone else and verify any qualifications with an independent trade body before hiring a contractor. Before beginning the work, conduct online research on the company and ensure that any written agreement, including the total cost, is in place.

You can also agree in advance with many utility companies on a password that will be used by anyone they send to your home to verify their identity.

Talk to your friends and relatives in advance if you think they might be at risk. Inform them not to invite anyone into their home and to immediately contact you (or another dependable individual) if they ever receive a visit from a salesperson.

Scam mail & offers

Numerous cons continue to be carried out using the postal service, despite the advent of the internet. Scams involving investments, phony wins in competitions or the lottery, and offers for products that do not exist are examples of these. Always be on guard because formal correspondence can frequently appear more genuine than email!

We all receive marketing correspondence, but be on the lookout for any that sound too good to be true or involve competitions you have not entered (especially if you must first send money to claim your "prize").To make them sound more exclusive, many of these letters may be addressed to you personally and include phrases like "guaranteed win" or an urgent deadline to encourage you to act quickly.

How can you stay away from these con artists?

On the off chance that you get any of these letters, receptacle them! Your information will be added to a list of victims and shared with other con artists if you respond to even one. If you respond to more than one, you could be bombarded with more.

Talk to any elderly or vulnerable friends or family members who might fall for this scam to make sure they don't open any unsolicited letters.

By registering with the **Mail Preference Service** and **opting out of the open electoral roll** in the United Kingdom, you can reduce the number of marketing emails you receive. You can also **register your information** with Royal Mail to request that they not send you junk mail without an address.

In the UK, the Financial Conduct Authority (FCA) has a great website for **identifying investment and pension fraud.** Check it out!

Crash for cash

While the aforementioned scams cause financial and emotional harm, “Crash for Cash” risks serious bodily harm.

In this car accident con, con artists deliberately cause an accident in order to make a claim on the victim’s insurance. They will abruptly and without warning slam on their brakes while driving in front of another vehicle, making it nearly impossible for the victim to avoid hitting the back of the other vehicle.

This could take place on a slip road off of a motorway, just before a pedestrian crossing where there aren’t any pedestrians, or at a junction where the con artist pulls out in front of a car. Since the driver who hits from behind is frequently deemed to be at fault, the con artists will often make the victim file a claim on their insurance, often with an injury claim as well.

If you think it’s a scam, what should you do in an accident?

When you’re in a crash, your adrenaline levels are high, making it hard to think clearly at times. However, if you can, try to keep the following in mind:

- If you don’t have a pen and paper on hand, use your phone to make a lot of **notes** about what happened. Include precise descriptions of what was said and who was involved.
- Make a list of everyone’s **contact information** and look for any **witnesses** (but keep in mind that these people could be part of the same gang if the crash was a scam).
- **Photograph** the scene as well as any damage to either vehicle.
- Even if you initially believe that it is your fault or the other driver tries to blame you, **you should not accept responsibility** for anything.
- If you are suspicious, insist on calling the **police**, but do not directly challenge the other driver about your suspicions.
- Inform your **insurance** company as soon as possible of your suspicions. Contact the **Insurance Fraud Bureau** and report the accident to their Cheatline if you’re in the UK.

What else can you do to stay away from this con?

In order to provide video evidence in the event of an accident, many motorists are now installing dash cams. These can assist insurers in determining actual liability and provide police with evidence in the event of a scam. If the con artist sees a camera, even it could stop you from being chosen as a victim.

The following driving tips from can assist you in avoiding these con artists:

- Make an effort to anticipate potential dangers by looking far ahead.
- Give the car in front plenty of room, especially at intersections and pedestrian crossings.
- Be careful about a vehicle in front driving unpredictably or dialing back for reasons unknown.
- Keep well out of their way if you think the brake lights on the car in front might not be working.
- Never take headlight flashing as a signal to proceed.
- When waiting at a junction, do not assume that a vehicle coming from the right and signaling to the left will turn. Wait and check.

Conclusion

Being conned can be painful. It can easily hurt our pride and make us look stupid, and it can also make us feel betrayed and disappointed when we find out that the person we were opening our hearts to and maybe hoping to have a future with didn't really exist.

Knowing that you are not alone is essential. Tens of thousands of people are defrauded annually by these con artists, who are extremely skilled at what they do.

For assistance, **get in touch with a victim support group** in your country; Many are well-prepared to assist victims of these scams and can offer moral and practical support.

Don't be ashamed to tell anyone that you've been affected; at least one close friend will be able to support you through it.

www.ingramcontent.com/pod-product-compliance
Lightning Source LLC
LaVergne TN
LVHW052055160826
845678LV00015B/3241

* 9 7 9 8 3 6 7 1 2 0 0 1 1 *